Believe and be Baptized

by

Victor Jack

Distributors to the trade:
Hughes & Coleman Ltd, Delta Close, Norwich NR6 6BG

Copies also available from:
VICTOR JACK, The Homestead, Drinkstone, Bury St. Edmunds. IP30 9TL

Printed by:
Selsey Press Ltd, 84 High Street, Selsey, Chichester, West Sussex PO20 0QH

THE AIMS OF THIS BOOKLET

1. To provide a **simple** explanation of baptism for those who are thinking about being baptized.

2. To put baptism into perspective by illustrating that it is part of the developing experience of a Christian, and not an end in itself. To show it should follow faith in Christ and lead to a life of active fellowship in the church.

3. To give ministers, elders and youth leaders a handbook to pass on, or to work through with those applying for baptism.

4. To help those asking for baptism to demonstrate that they are ready for this step by writing answers to the questions in the book.

5. To provide parents with a straight-forward explanation of baptism, when they fail to understand the desires of their sons or daughters.

FOOTNOTE: All quotations from the Bible are from the New International Version

BELIEVE AND BE BAPTIZED

The message Peter preached on the day of Pentecost shows us the milestones we need to pass on our journey to faith in Jesus Christ. The results that followed his preaching teach us the way to enjoy the rich fellowship of the church. It is an exciting journey which gets more rewarding the further we travel. Let us begin by reading carefully Acts 2.22-47, because this will form a basis for most of what follows.

"Men of Israel, listen to this: Jesus of Nazareth was a man accredited by God to you by miracles, wonders and signs, which God did among you through him, as you yourselves know. This man was handed over to you by God's set purpose and foreknowledge; and you, with the help of wicked men, put him to death by nailing him to the cross. But God raised him from the dead, freeing him from the agony of death, because it was impossible for death to keep its hold on him. David said about him:
'I saw the Lord always before me.
Because he is at my right hand,
I will not be shaken.
Therefore my heart is glad and
my tongue rejoices;
my body also will live in hope,
because you will not abandon me to the grave,
nor will you let your Holy One see decay.
You have made known to me the paths of life;
you will fill me with joy in your presence'.

Brothers, I can tell you confidently that the patriarch David died and was buried, and his tomb is here to this day. But he was a prophet and knew that God had promised him on oath that he would place one of his descendants on his throne. Seeing what was ahead, he spoke of the resurrection of the Christ, that he was not abandoned to the grave, nor did his body see decay. God has raised this Jesus to life, and we are all witnesses of the fact. Exalted to the right hand of God, he has received from the Father the promised Holy Spirit and has poured out what you now see and hear. For David did not ascend to heaven, and yet he said,
'The Lord said to my Lord:
"Sit at my right hand
until I make your enemies
a footstool for your feet."'
Therefore let all Israel be assured of this: God has made this Jesus, whom you crucified, both Lord and Christ."

When the people heard this, they were cut to the heart and said to Peter and the other apostles, "Brothers, what shall we do?"

Peter replied, "Repent and be baptized, every one of you, in the name of Jesus Christ so that your sins may be forgiven. And you will receive the gift of the Holy Spirit. The promise is for you and your children and for all who are far off — for all whom the Lord our God will call."

With many other words he warned them; and he pleaded with them, "Save yourselves from this corrupt generation." Those who accepted his message were baptized, and about three thousand were added to their number that day.

They devoted themselves to the apostles' teaching and to the fellowship, to the breaking of bread and to prayer. Everyone was filled with awe, and many wonders and miraculous signs were done by the apostles. All the believers were together and had everything in common. Selling their possessions and goods, they gave to anyone as he had need. Every day they continued to meet together in the temple courts. They broke bread in their homes and ate together with glad and sincere hearts, praising God and enjoying the favour of all the people. And the Lord added to their number daily those who were being saved." Acts 2.22-47.

Many different pictures have been used to illustrate what it means both to become a Christian and also to live the Christian life. We could take some from the Bible such as a walk, a race and a battle. In this study, however, we shall use the picture of crossing a river by means of stepping stones in order to emphasise how easy it is, after setting out, to get marooned mid-stream and make no further progress. God's blessing and

our spiritual progress are then forfeited. Just as it takes effort and courage at times to leap from one stone to another, so there are many challenging steps to take if we are to keep moving forward as Christians. One of these is baptism, with its requirement that we come out into the open and boldly declare our allegiance to Jesus Christ. Baptism is the main subject of this booklet, because too many get stranded here. There is always a price to pay in following Christ but the reward outweighs the cost.

Before considering the importance of baptism, let us first trace the steps that lead up to it. This will help to make sure that we are ready to be baptized. We might call the first stepping-stone:—

STEP ONE:— CONFRONTED WITH THE TRUTH

In his message Peter confronted the people with the truth about themselves. It is worth looking at some of the facts Peter presented because they still apply today.

THE TRUTH ABOUT JESUS CHRIST

His Life Jesus was more than a man, He was the Son of God, the promised Messiah. Peter declared "Jesus of Nazareth was a man accredited by God to you by miracles, wonders and signs, which God did among you through him, as you yourselves know." (v.22)

His Death This was no accident but part of God's plan for our salvation. "This man was handed over to you by God's set purpose and foreknowl-

5

edge; and you, with the help of wicked men, put him to death by nailing him to the cross." (v.23)

His Resurrection Men crucified Him "but God raised him from the dead, freeing him from the agony of death, because it was impossible for death to keep its hold on him." (v.24) The Prince of life conquered the Prince of death. Unlike other great leaders of the past, Jesus Christ is alive today.

His Exaltation Jesus was "exalted to the right hand of God" (v.33) and waits the time when God's promise will be fulfilled, "sit at my right hand until I make your enemies a footstool for your feet" (vs.34,35). The time is coming when He will rule the world in peace and righteousness, and everyone will know that He is Lord to the glory of God.

A fuller picture of who Jesus is and what He came to do is found in two wonderful paragraphs in the New Testament. Read and meditate on Philippians 2.5-11 and Colossians 1.15-23.

THE TRUTH ABOUT THEMSELVES

They were **SINNERS**, guilty of the death of Jesus Christ (vs.23,36). We too are guilty, for we are a part of the sinful human race for whom Jesus Christ died. God's verdict on us all is unmistakably clear. "There is no-one righteous, not even one; there is no-one who understands, no-one who seeks God. All have turned away, they have together become worthless; there is no-one who does good, not even one." (Romans 3.10-12)

In our hearts we know the Bible is right when it states "for all have sinned and fall short of the glory of God." (Romans 3.23)

They must **REPENT** in order to be forgiven and receive the gift of the Holy Spirit. So must we. "Repent and be baptized, everyone of you, in the name of Jesus Christ so that your sins may be forgiven. And you will receive the gift of the Holy Spirit." (v.38) Jesus taught "unless you repent, you too will all perish" (Luke 13.3,5). Paul declared, God "commands all people everywhere to repent. For he has set a day when he will judge the world with justice by the man he has appointed" (Acts 17.30,31).

They must **CALL** on the name of the Lord for salvation, 'Lord, save me' must be the cry of our hearts. "And everyone who calls on the name of the Lord will be saved" (v.21)

They must be **BAPTIZED.** "Repent and be baptized, everyone of you, in the name of Jesus Christ." (v.38) We too must be baptized in order to show that our past has been buried and that we have begun a new life in Christ.

STEP TWO:— CONVICTED BY THE TRUTH

In the next paragraph we discover how the listening crowd reacted to Peter's message "when the people heard this, they were cut to the heart" (v.37). Peter's message went to their consciences like an arrow to its mark. The truth 'hit home'. Much preaching goes straight over people's heads, but this was right on target. The people understood what they heard, their consciences were awakened and they knew themselves to be guilty. The Spirit of God drove the word of God home into the hearts of the hearers in such a supernatural way that it caused them to face up to their responsibilities before God.

Many people obviously get marooned on the first stepping stone. They are not convicted when confronted with the truth. It is so easy to harden our hearts whenever the truth about God is preached, and to silence the work of the Holy Spirit who seeks to open our minds and hearts to the Lord Jesus. Whenever this message is preached, it produces one of three results: it is rejected, neglected or accepted.

Conviction of sin is like an alarm clock which rings and rings in our conscience until we rise from our sleepy state and respond to its call. We may try to send our conscience back to sleep, we may try to silence its inner voice, but we shall not know God's forgiveness and peace until we obey the message His Holy Spirit has impressed on our hearts.

STEP THREE:— CONCERNED ABOUT THE TRUTH

Peter's listeners cried out "Brothers, what shall we do?" (v.37) The truth they heard enlightened their minds, awakened their consciences and now challenged their hearts. Their cry is full of anxious enquiry. To whom could they turn? How could they quieten their troubled spirits? Where could they find the peace of God? Peter pointed them to Jesus Christ. Those who know they are sick consult a doctor, and those who

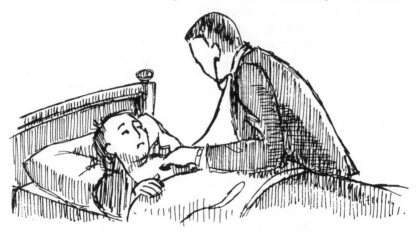

know they have sinned against God must turn to Jesus Christ, the Great Physician. Jesus said "It is not the healthy who need a doctor, but the sick. I have not come to call the righteous, but sinners to repentance." (Lk. 5.31,32)

STEP FOUR:— CONVERTED TO JESUS CHRIST

In answer to their question "What shall we do?" Peter said "Repent and be baptized every one of you in the name of Jesus Christ so that your sins may be forgiven. And you will receive the gift of the Holy Spirit." Those listening would know exactly what he meant because John the Baptist had preached the necessity of repentance and then baptized those that turned to God. The people responded readily to this direct challenge.

There are three pictures used in this passage to illustrate the meaning of becoming a Christian. It will be helpful to look at them in order to make sure that we really belong to Jesus Christ and are therefore ready for the step of baptism.

REPENTING

Repentance means to have a change of mind that leads to a change of direction, or put simply, to turn from ourselves and our sin to God.

Repentance is a basic and essential part of the message of the New Testament. John the Baptist preached "Repent, for the kingdom of heaven is near." (Matt.3.1-2) Jesus began His ministry with the words "repent, for the kingdom of heaven is near" (Matt.4.17). Peter declared in another sermon "Repent, then, and turn to God, so that your sins may be wiped out" (Act 3.19)

We have all wandered away from God and taken the pathway in life that suited us best. We need to turn around and leave what Jesus called the "broad road that leads to destruction" and take the "narrow road that leads to life". (Matt.7.13,14) This is repentance and is well illustrated by the military command "Halt, about turn, quick march." Stop and think about how you are living. Do an about turn, leave your way and start following the way of Christ.

Repentance is much more than saying that we are sorry. It means **showing** that we are, by the changed life we live. We cannot follow Jesus Christ without forsaking sin. Repentance means 'to leave the sin I loved before and show that I'm in earnest by doing so no more'.

CALLING

"And everyone who calls on the name of the Lord will be saved" (v.21). Many needy people called on Jesus Christ for help during his life-time. He heard and answered their cry. None of them was disappointed.

"A man with leprosy came to him and begged him on his knees 'If you are willing, you can make me clean'. Filled with compassion, Jesus reached out his hand and touched the man. 'I am willing' he said 'Be clean!' Immediately the leprosy left him and he was cured." (Mark 1.40-42)

When blind Bartimaeus heard that Jesus was going down the road where he was sitting and begging "he began to shout 'Jesus, Son of David, have mercy on me!' 'Go' said Jesus 'your faith has healed you'. Immediately he received his sight and followed Jesus along the road." (Mark 10.46-52)

The promise of Jesus still holds good today. If we call on him we will be saved, which means to be delivered from the power and penalty of sin.

RECEIVING

In verse 41 we read that the crowd "accepted his message" or "received his word". (RSV) The people were willing, not only to receive God's word from Peter's lips, but also willing to receive Jesus Christ as their Lord and Master, as is obvious by all that follows in the chapter. **Believing** and **receiving** are two key words to remember when we think of becoming a Christian. We believe the truth about Jesus Christ and then allow Him to take control of our lives. "Yet to all who received him, to those who believed in his name, he gave the right to become children of God." (Jn.1.12)

Peter also promised that those who repented would "receive the gift of the Holy Spirit" (v.38). Every person who becomes a Christian is given the Holy Spirit to enable them to live the Christian life. To try and live the Christian life without the Holy Spirit is like trying to drive a car without any fuel in the tank. We will have neither the desire nor the power to live for the glory of God.

God gives us the Holy Spirit so that we have the inward assurance that we are His children and He is our Father. "The Spirit himself testifies with our spirit that we are God's children". (Rom. 8.16) "By him we cry 'Abba Father' " (Rom. 8.15)

God gives us the Holy Spirit so that we can understand the Bible. The Holy Spirit who inspired the writing of Scripture also interprets it. Jesus promised that the Holy Spirit would "teach you all things and will remind you of everything I have said to you" (Jn.14.26). He later added "when he, the Spirit of truth, comes, he will guide you into all truth."

God gives us the Holy Spirit so that we can be bold in our witness as Christians. In Acts 4.31 we read "they were all filled with the Holy Spirit and spoke the word of God boldly."

Can we honestly say that we have repented before God, trusted Jesus Christ by faith, and received the Holy Spirit into our lives. If the answer is 'Yes', then we are ready and need to be willing to obey His command to be baptized. Too many get sidetracked just here. They are converted, but do not continue to progress. Conversion is only the beginning. It is a gateway through which we pass to a completely new area of life. having begun we must continue. Having responded to the call to believe we must now obey the command to be baptized.

QUESTIONS TO ANSWER

1. List the important truths Peter taught the people about Jesus on the day of Pentecost.

....

....

....

....

2. Write down the 2 commands and the 2 promises Peter gave to the people in Acts 2.38.

....

....

....

3. Explain the meaning of repentance in your own words.

....

....

....

4. Outline some of the ways in which the Holy Spirit helps us in our Christian lives.

....

....

....

5. Give a brief account of how your became a Christian

....

....

....

....

6. In what ways have you been helped to grow as a Christian?

....

....

....

....

STEP FIVE:— CONFESSING JESUS CHRIST

Those who accepted his message **were baptized'** (v.41). Having bcome Christians, they were willing to show others that they belonged to Jesus Christ. We must not remain secret disciples as though we were afraid of what others might think, or were ashamed of our new way of life. We need to be bold about our faith in Jesus Christ, and proud of our allegiance to Him. He said "If anyone is ashamed of me and my words in this adulterous and sinful generation, the Son of Man will be ashamed of him when he comes in his Father's glory with the holy angels." (Mk.8.38). There are three ways in which we can confess Jesus Christ.

BY OUR LIPS

"If you confess with your mouth, 'Jesus is Lord', and believe in your heart that God raised him from the dead, you will be saved. For it is with your heart that you believe and are justified, and it is with your mouth that you confess and are saved." (Rom.10.9,10)

Let us use our lips to tell our friends of Jesus Christ and of all He has done for us. It will take a little courage at first, but we can go on to do this confidently.

BY OUR LIVES

If we tell others that we are Christians, we must be careful to live like Christians, otherwise we shall be called hypocrites. "Whatever happens, conduct yourselves in a manner worthy of the gospel of Christ."

(Phil.1.27) "I urge you to live a life worthy of the calling you have received." (Eph.4.1)

A changed life is always a powerful witness. People may misunderstand or misinterpret our words, but they will always notice our actions. What we do is as important as what we say.

The witness of our lives resembles a bright light in a dark world. Jesus Christ said "Let you light shine before men, that they may see your good deeds and praise your Father in heaven." (Matt.5.16)

"Do everything without complaining or arguing, so that you may become blameless and pure, children of God without fault in a crooked and depraved generation, in which you **shine like stars** in the universe." (Phil. 2.14,15)

BY BEING BAPTIZED

Baptism is another courageous way of confessing our faith in Jesus Christ. Baptism might almost be called 'The badge of discipleship'. Just as people may wear a badge to identify themselves with a certain movement, so we may look upon baptism as a way of showing people that we belong to Jesus Christ. That is one of the reasons why we are baptized "in the name of the Father and of the Son and of the Holy Spirit" (Matt.28.19). This indicates not only to whom we belong but also under whose authority we live. There is more in it than that, as we shall see; but before we look at the meaning of baptism there are two points that need to be emphasised.

Baptism Follows Belief in Jesus Christ

This is a simple but very important principle that is stressed again and again in the New Testament. We must be committed to Jesus Christ before we can think of confessing Jesus Christ in baptism, otherwise we are putting the cart before the horse. A few verses from the Bible will help to impress this upon our minds. Jesus said "Go into all the world and preach the good news to all creation. Whoever **believes** and is baptized will be saved, but whoever does not believe will be condemned." (Mk.16.15,16) "But when they **believed** Philip as he preached the good news of the kingdom of God and the name of Jesus Christ, they were baptized, both men and women. Simon himself **believed** and was baptized." (Acts 8. 12,13) ". . . and many of the Corinthians who heard him **believed** and were baptized." (Acts 18.8)

To baptize a person who has never become a true Christian is like dressing a man in uniform and declaring him to be a soldier when he has never enlisted in the army. Unless we have personally believed in Christ, we have no faith to confess in baptism. If we are baptized without a true commitment to Christ we make the rite of baptism meaningless.

Baptism Cannot Produce Salvation

Although baptism is often linked with salvation, the Bible never suggests that we can experience a spiritual change of heart by being baptized. A person is not baptized to **make** him a Christian, but rather to show he **is** a Christian. Anything that may be done to us **outwardly**, cannot change us **inwardly,** so far as God is concerned. There are no magical powers in the water. Water can cleanse the hands but not the heart.

In his first epistle, Peter links baptism with salvation and uses Noah's ark and the flood as an illustration. He states that baptism is "not the removal of dirt from the body, but the pledge of a good conscience towards God. It saves you by the resurrection of Jesus Christ, who has gone into heaven and is at God's right hand." (1 Pet.3.20-22) Although the flood bore the ark to safety, Noah and his family were saved through being in the ark. We are saved through being 'in Christ', not through the waters of baptism.

Unfortunately, some think that through being baptized as children, they automatically become Christians. Their faith is in a particular religious rite, rather than in the work of Jesus Christ. Always in Scripture salvation is by grace through faith and not by any work, whether it be a good deed we perform or a rite to which we submit. "For it is by grace you have been saved, through faith – and this is not from yourselves, it is the gift of God – not by works, so that no-one can boast." (Eph.2.8,9)

BAPTISM AND ITS MEANING

Why is it necessary to be baptized? What does it signify? In baptism we actively and openly make declaration of certain facts.

1. OUR OBEDIENCE TO JESUS CHRIST

Baptism was part of the great commission that Jesus Christ gave to His disciples before He ascended to heaven "go and make disciples of all nations, baptizing them in the name of the Father and of the Son and of the Holy Spirit, and teaching them to **obey** everything I have commanded you." (Matt.28.19,20) They were under divine orders. As we read through the book of Acts, we see how implicitly those orders were obeyed. Every new Christian was baptized. In Acts 10.48 we discover that Peter "**ordered** that they be baptized" which illustrates that neither the apostles nor the new believers regarded baptism as an optional extra.

If it is the will of Jesus Christ that every person who becomes a Christian should be baptized, then we must bow in submission to His will. We must obey Him, not grudgingly but willingly. Before we became Christians, we thought only of pleasing ourselves, now we must make it our goal to please Him. (2 Cor.5.9)

The One to whom we have given our lives is Jesus Christ the Lord. Each name is significant. Jesus is the Saviour, because He died for me. Christ is the Living One, who has come to live in me. He is Lord, which means that He is owner, master and king. If He is my owner, I am His personal property. If He is my king I should be His loyal subject. The One who died for me, and lives in me, should rule over me.

The whole question of our obedience to Jesus Christ is really a test of our love for Him. How willing are we to do what He wants? He said "If you love me, you will obey what I command." (Jn.14.15) Obedience that does not spring from love is a cold and clinical response.

Jesus also said "You are my friends if you do what I command." (Jn.15.14) Nothing will foster our friendship with Jesus Christ more than willing obedience. When we discover and obey His will, this will bring an added joy to our Christian experience. He said "Now that you know these things, you will be blessed if you do them." (Jn.13.17)   "... what are you waiting for? Get up, be baptized . . ." (Acts 22.16)

2.   OUR CONFESSION OF JESUS CHRIST

Baptism has been described as 'an outward sign of an inward faith.' This is a simple but helpful definition. Faith is an invisible, intangible thing and needs to be expressed in action. We can show people what they cannot see; we can declare what they may not have already guessed, that our faith is in Jesus Christ.

Some persons become Christians after going to the front of a church in response to an appeal. Many others make a personal and private commitment to Jesus Christ when they are quite alone. They do not always tell someone else about it (which is a pity), though others may guess. No one is really sure where they stand until they come out into the open and are baptized. A young man may become a police cadet, without telling anyone. People will only know he belongs

to the police force when they see him proudly wearing his uniform. We should be equally proud that we belong to Jesus Christ. Baptism is a way of 'getting into uniform', a wearing of the Master's colours. Too many seem almost ashamed of their faith; they are not open enough about it.

> 'Ashamed to be a Christian!
> Afraid the world should know
> I'm on the way to Heaven
> Where joys eternal flow!
> Afraid to wear Thy colours,
> Or blush to follow Thee!
> Forbid it, O my Saviour,
> That I should ever be.'

Paul said "I am not ashamed of the gospel!" (Rom. 1.16). Jesus Christ said "whoever acknowledges me before men, I will also acknowledge him before my Father in heaven. But whoever disowns

me before men, I will disown him before my Father in heaven."
(Mt.10.32,33)

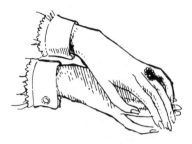

When a girl is engaged, her fiancé gives her a ring, so that she can indicate to others that her life is linked with his. What does she do with this outward sign of her inward attachment? Does she keep it secretly in its little box? Of course not! The ring is proudly worn on the hand for all to see. Let us be equally glad to confess that our lives belong to Jesus Christ. ". . . what are you waiting for? Get up, be baptized . . ." (Act 22.16)

3. OUR DEDICATION TO JESUS CHRIST

The oath sworn by a Roman soldier to the Emperor, when he declared his allegiance to him was called in Latin, the sacramentum. It was something the soldier did after enlisting. In this way he committed himself to a life of loyalty and dedicated service to the Emperor.

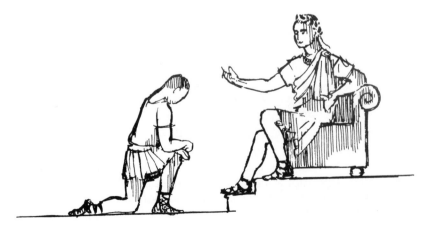

The two ordinances, baptism and the Lord's supper, which Jesus gave His disciples whereby they could show their allegiance to Him, were soon known as 'sacraments'.

A sacrament seals a promise made. God promised Noah that He would not bring a similar flood on the earth again. He then gave the outward sign of the bow in the cloud to seal the promise made (Gen. 9.8-17). Similarly in a marriage service, the husband, having promised to forsake all others and give himself to his wife alone as long as they live, seals this solemn pledge by placing a ring on her finger.

We promised to follow Jesus Christ when we became Christians and we ought to look upon baptism as a step of dedication. We must not take this step lightly. We must be true to our vow. It will mean leaving behind the things that grieve Jesus Christ and giving ourselves devotedly to Him. Separation from all we know to be wrong and dedication to Jesus Christ go hand in hand. "Do not offer the parts of your body to sin, as instruments of wickedness, but rather offer yourselves to God, as those who have been brought from death to life; and offer the parts of your body to him as instruments of righteousness." (Rom.6.13) The step of baptism needs to be taken thoughtfully and seriously. We should regard it as an act of total dedication to our Lord and Master, an offering of our life to Him for all time. "Therefore, I urge you, brothers, in view of God's mercy, to offer your bodies as living sacrifices, holy and pleasing to God — which is your spiritual worship." (Rom.12.1)

It would be serious for a Roman soldier to go back on his oath and desert the ranks. It is very sad when the marriage vows are broken. It is a tragedy when a Christian goes back to his old way of life. Let us determine, God helping us, never to turn back. Jesus Christ said "No-one who puts his hand to the plough and looks back is fit for service in the kingdom of God." (Lk.9.62)   Satan will contest our dedication to Jesus Christ all the way by fierce temptation, bitter disappointments, and even persecution.

In some countries today, Christians have to face imprisonment following baptism: it is really costly for them to take this step. We are never alone in these experiences. The Lord Jesus will stand by us and strengthen us. "... what are you waiting for? Get up, be baptized ..." (Acts 22.16)

4.   OUR IDENTIFICATION WITH JESUS CHRIST

This is the main and deeper meaning of baptism, which is brought out in the teaching of the apostles. The origin of Christian baptism is found in the gospels, the practice of it in the book of Acts and the explanation of it in the Epistles. The main passage which deals with this aspect is Rom. 6.3-14.

In baptism we are identified with Jesus Christ in His three great acts that secured our salvation — His death, burial and resurrection. Paul sums up the Christian message by linking these together "Christ died for our sins . . . He was buried . . . He was raised on the third day . . ." (1 Cor. 15.3,4).

His Identification With Us

The Lord Jesus first came and identified Himself with sinners before He called sinners to identify themselves with Him. He did this in two ways: (1) **By His Baptism in Jordan** John baptized in Jordan those who repented in response to his preaching. When Jesus Christ asked to be baptized, John at first refused. This was because John knew that Jesus had no need of repentance. Jesus went down into the water in order to stand in the sinner's place. He identified Himself with them in their relation to God as sinners. His baptism in Jordan was also a picture of His death, and His coming up from the water a portrayal of His resurrection. (2) **By His Baptism On The Cross** Jesus Christ said "I have a baptism to undergo, and how distressed I am until it is completed!" (Lk.12.50). Jesus was referring to the time when He would be overwhelmed by mental agony, physical pain, and spiritual anguish, on the cross. He was immersed in suffering as He bore God's judgement on man's sin. In His life and in His death, Jesus, who was sinless, took the place of those who were sinful.

'He took the guilty sinner's place
And suffered in his stead,
For man — O miracle of grace
For man, the Saviour bled.'

Our Identification With Him

When we became Christians, two things happened, Our old way of life finished. A completely new way of life began. This is summed up by two

21

expressions "count yourselves **dead to sin** and **alive to God** in Christ Jesus." (Rom.6.11) and "therefore, if anyone is in Christ, he is a new creation; **the old** has gone, **the new** has come!" (2 Cor.5.17) The moment our lives were linked with Christ, the two things that happened to Him, happened also to us. We died with Him to sin and its power over us, and we rose with Him to a new life. These great truths are clearly demonstrated in baptism by immersion.

Into the Water — DEATH As we go down into the water, we are saying in effect, that just as Jesus Christ died for our sin on the cross, so we have died to sin in our lives. There has been a complete break with the past — a death — "count yourselves **dead to sin**" (Rom.6.11) This is not the place for a doctrinal study of the truth behind the phrase 'dead to sin' but its practical meaning is important and clear. If a person is so engrossed in reading the newspaper that all attempts to divert his attention fail, then we could say 'He is dead to the world'. By this we mean that he is insensitive to, or not conscious of our attempts to entice him away from the newspaper. We need to be so absorbed in our rich friendship with Jesus Christ, that the temptations of the Enemy pass us by.

Under The Water — BURIAL A dead person must be buried. Just as Jesus Christ was buried in the tomb, so when we are lowered beneath the water our lives as sinners are regarded as put out of sight. The Bible teaches "we were therefore buried with him through baptism into death" (Rom.6.4.) Our baptism then becomes a kind of funeral, and the water a grave, by which a declaration is made to all that the sinner has been committed to death. Death followed by burial now prevents our returning to our former way of life. This is why Paul asks the question "We died to sin; how can we live in it any longer?" (Rom.6.2.)

Out Of The Water — RESURRECTION "We were therefore buried with him through baptism into death in order that, just as Christ was raised from the dead through the glory of the Father, we too may live a new life. If we have been united with Him in his death, we will certainly also be united with him in his resurrection." (Rom.6.4,5)

Jesus Christ was raised from the dead by the power of God. We are lifted from the water to live a new and distinctive life, the life of Christ Himself. As Paul explained it "I have been crucified with Christ and I no longer live, but Christ lives in me. The life I live in the body, I live by faith in the Son of God, who loved me and gave himself for me." (Gal.2.20)

The life we live as Christians must express these two great truths, that we are dead to sin and alive to God. An illustration from nature will help us to see this more clearly. Some flowers close up at night when the darkness falls, but open out when morning breaks and the sun shines. They are dead to the dark and alive to the light, closed to one sphere but open to the other. In the Bible, darkness is often linked with evil and light with purity. Jesus Christ said "men loved darkness instead of light, because their deeds were evil" (Jn.3.19) and "I am the light of the world. Whoever follows me will never walk in darkness, but will have the light of

life." (Jn.8.12) Like the flowers, our lives must be closed to those things which we know are dark and evil, and wide open to the light and love of God.(Rom.6.11)

To walk in newness of life is a continual challenge. Every day we sense the downward pull of our sinful natures, but every day we may also experience the inward power of Jesus Christ lifting us up. We must not rely upon past experiences, such as conversion and baptism, wonderful as they are; we must depend upon a day by day experience of Jesus Christ living His life through us. Without this we shall fail, because the Enemy is too strong for us. Unfortunately, when some are baptized they seem to think they have reached the end of the road; in reality it is only part of the beginning. Those who became Christians in the New Testament were nearly always baptized immediately, so their knowledge and experience of Jesus Christ was just commencing. In Acts 2 the new converts did not stand still after being baptized, they moved on to the things that would build up their faith. This brings us to the next stepping stone, which deals with our progress as Christians.

QUESTIONS TO ANSWER

1. List 3 ways in which we can show others that we are Christians.

....

....

....

....

....

2. Write out two of the verses that indicate baptism should follow belief in Christ.

....

....

....

....

3. Write a note on the place of obedience in relation to baptism.

....

....

....

4. Why should the step of baptism be taken seriously?

....

....

....

5. What are we declaring in the following 3 actions in our baptism?
   a. Into the water

....

....

   b. Under the water

....

....

   c. Out of the water

....

....

To think over   Is there any good reason why I should not obey the command of Christ to be baptized?

STEP SIX: CONTINUING WITH JESUS CHRIST

"Those who accepted his message were baptized, and about three thousand were added to their number that day. They devoted themselves to the apostles' teaching and to the fellowship, to the breaking of bread and to prayer." (Acts 2.41,42) The apostles taught the new Christians the next steps in the Christian life, and the converts immediately became involved in the worship and witness of the Christian church. This is the secret of progress.

Jesus Christ sent the disciples into the world to preach the gospel and to baptize those who would believe. He then added "teaching them to obey everything I have commanded you" (Mt.28.20) Preaching the Gospel, baptizing the converts and teaching the commandments of Jesus Christ sums up the work of the Christian church. The first section of this booklet dealt with believing the gospel, the second with being baptized, and the third deals with the continuing life of the Christian. Being baptized then is not an end in itself, but a part of the developing life of the Christian. Here are four vital things to which we need to devote ourselves.

THE APOSTLES' TEACHING

Jesus Christ spent three years teaching His disciples before sending them into the world to teach others. The things they taught the people by word of mouth are written down for us in the New Testament. If therefore we are to devote ourselves to the apostles' teaching it will be necessary for us to do three things. With a Bible open before us let us:

(a) **Read It Regularly** Time needs to be set aside each day for thoughtful reading of God's Word. Only in this way can we feed ourselves and grow strong spiritually. The Bible is our food, and if we neglect to read it, our faith will wither and even die. Make sure you have some Scripture Union notes to guide you in your readings. It will be necessary, not only to read the Bible quietly by ourselves, but also to read it regularly with others in home groups and church services, where the meaning of God's Word is explained. Only in this way can we build up our faith and discover God's will for our lives. 'Enquire within about everything' are good words to write inside your Bible, because all we need for daily living is contained in this divine book. 'It contains light to direct you, food to support you, comfort to cheer you and armour to protect you. It is the traveller's map, the pilgrim's staff, the pilot's compass, the soldier's sword and the Christian's charter.'

(b) **Interpret It Prayerfully**   We must not think of reading the Bible merely as an academic exercise, but think primarily of how we can prayerfully interpret its teachings, applying them to our daily lives. Before reading it is good to pray "Open my eyes that I may see wonderful things in your law." (Ps.119.18) By ourselves we shall not understand all that we read, we need the help of the Holy Spirit. When we have taken in a part of God's Word, it is good to go back and pray over it asking the Holy Spirit to interpret it to us. It's a good discipline to look for a promise to claim, an

example to follow, a warning to heed, a command to obey. In this way we can relate God's Word to our own lives.

(c)   **Obey It Continually** It is so easy to fail to put into practice the things we learn from the Bible. This is sin. "Anyone, then, who knows the good he ought to do and doesn't do it, sins." (Jas.4.17) "Do not merely listen to the word, and so deceive yourselves. Do what it says." (Jas.1.22) To obey God is often costly, but He will always provide the strength to do what He asks.

To devote ourselves to the apostles' teaching is to cling to the Word of God, especially when we are being tested. Paul said to Timothy "continue in what you have learned and have become convinced of" (2 Tim.3.14). Jesus Christ said "if you hold to my teaching, you are really my disciples." (Jn.8.31)

FELLOWSHIP

Fellowship simply means 'to have a share in something with someone'. Christian fellowship refers to the close and intimate relationship people share both with Jesus Christ and with one another. The early Christians thrived on this deep sense of friendship as they worshipped together, witnessed together, prayed together and enjoyed Christ together. They shared in each other's joys and sorrows. They helped and encouraged one another. In Acts 2.44-46, we get a clear picture of the common life they enjoyed. They were bound together by the invisible bond of Christ's love, which was the source of their unity and strength, especially in days of persecution. It has been said 'blood ties are the strongest ties'. This is particularly true amongst Christians who realise they have been purchased by the precious blood of Christ. There are two aspects of fellowship we need to develop.

(a) **Fellowship With Christ** In 1 Cor.1.9 we read "God who has called you into fellowship with his Son Jesus Christ our Lord is faithful." God has called us to share in the life of His Son, which means we can continually experience His joy and peace and strength in our lives. This is something we need to develop, so that our fellowship with Him grows stronger. It is rewarding to discover that the closer we get to Jesus Christ the closer we want to get, and the deeper our friendship becomes the deeper we want it to be. After many years on the Christian pathway, Paul's great longing still was "I want to know Christ." (Phil.3.10)

Through his death on the cross Jesus Christ has made it possible for us to know true fellowship with God, and with Himself. As a magnet draws iron filings to itself, so the magnetism of Christ's love has drawn us to Himself. Jesus Christ said "But I, when I am lifted up from the earth, will draw all men to myself." (Jn.12.32) As we enjoy the privilege of fellowship with Christ, let us remember with grateful hearts the price He paid.

(b) Fellowship With Others John speaks not only of "fellowship with the Father and with His Son Jesus Christ" (1 Jn.1.3) but refers also to having 'fellowship with one another'. (1 Jn. 1.7) This arises out of and depends upon our fellowship with God. Jesus Christ has not only drawn us close to Himself but united us as Christians to each other. We are members of a large and wonderful family with Christ as the Head. We belong, not only to Christ but also to one another. Just as the spokes of a bicycle wheel are joined to the hub at the centre and to the rim at the circumference; so each Christian is joined to Christ, who is the centre of our fellowship, and joined also to every other believer in the

wider circle of Christian fellowship. As individual Christians, 'spokes in the wheel', we must make sure that we retain continual contact with Christ and close contact with Christians in order to maintain spiritual vitality and the unity of Christian fellowship. Trouble begins when the spoke comes adrift at either end.

No Christian was ever meant to go it alone. We need to spend time with Jesus Christ and with others of like mind. 'Birds of a feather flock together' and Christians need to keep together or the pressures of the world and the opposition of Satan will weaken our faith. This means every Christian needs to belong to a place of worship where God's word is faithfully preached, and attend regularly the services that are arranged. "Let us not give up meeting together, as some are in the habit of doing, but let us encourage one another – and all the more as you see

the Day approaching." (Heb. 10.25) If we stay away from Christian fellowship our love for the Lord Jesus will soon cool off, just as a piece of coal taken out of a fire and placed on the hearth soon becomes cold and dead. To be in the company of keen Christians is like being in the centre of a fire, because when we are together, with Jesus Christ in the midst, He kindles a fire of love in our hearts which generates warm Christian fellowship.

It is a great privilege to belong to a group of Christians, but it carries with it the responsibility of doing all we can to contribute to the smooth running and spiritual well-being of the fellowship. It will demand time, effort and money if it is going to be maintained and increased. Let us be careful not to divide and spoil the fellowship by unkind words or selfish actions. Satan loves to weaken the effectiveness of Christians by splitting them up into little groups.

BREAKING OF BREAD

To eat together has always been a sign of fellowship, especially in the East, but the term used here 'breaking of bread' means something more than simply sharing an ordinary meal. It refers to the Lord's Supper or the communion service. Jesus Christ took bread and wine, the two most common elements of an Eastern meal, and used them as a picture of His body and His blood. By breaking bread together, the disciples were doing what Jesus Christ had asked. He instituted and requested this before He died, in order that they might keep Him continually in their minds. Every Christian should do the same.

(1) **Instituted by Jesus Christ** (Mt.26.26-30; Mk.14.22-25; Lk.22.19-20; 1 Cor.11.23-32) On the very night in which Jesus Christ was betrayed, He was eating a meal with His disciples in the upper room. While they were eating, He took a loaf of bread, gave thanks, broke it and distributed it amongst the disciples saying "This is my body given for you; do this in remembrance of me." He also took a cup of wine, and after giving thanks passed it to His disciples saying "this cup is the new covenant in my blood, which is poured out for you." (Lk.22.20). The disciples would not at that time have understood the full significance of what Jesus Christ had said and done, but He knew the painful truth. He had come to give His body and shed His Life's blood for the sins of the world, and therefore took the simple elements of bread and wine to portray these profound truths.

(2) **Requested By Jesus Christ** Jesus Christ requested His disciples to continue regularly the simple service He had begun, in remembrance

of Himself. When He instituted the service, He said "do this in remembrance of me". The words 'do this' are in the present continuous tense, which means 'keep on doing this' until I come again. If we have obeyed the command of Jesus Christ in being baptized, we must also respond to His request that we break bread in memory of Him. These are the only two ordinances Christ gave us.

He knew just how forgetful we would be and how prone to stray from Him, so He instituted this simple but powerful visual aid. It reminds us continually of the great price He paid to free us from sin.
Let us be in our place at this important and lovely communion service as often as possible or our hearts will grow cold and we will forget to thank the One who died to give us life.

PRAYERS

Those that believed and were baptized "devoted themselves to prayer." (Acts 2.42) The fourth activity in which the new converts continued steadfastly is described as 'the prayers'. (RSV) This indicates they had set times when they met together for united prayer. Private prayer is vital to the spiritual life of the individual while public and corporate prayer is essential for the spiritual well-being of any fellowship. Prayer has been likened to breathing. Without it there cannot be life or growth.

(a) **Private Prayer** This was taught by Jesus Christ. "When you pray, go into your room, close the door and pray to your Father, who is unseen. Then your Father who sees what is done in secret will reward you." (Mt. 6.6) This was also practised by Jesus Christ. It is reported of Him that "very early in the morning, while it was still dark, Jesus got up, left the house and went off to a solitary place, where he prayed." (Mk. 1.35) If Jesus Christ found it necessary to pray, how much more should we. It has been said "The secret of prayer is prayer in secret" and those who have put this principle to work have found it to be true.

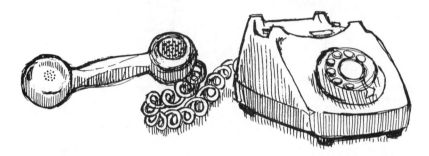

Prayer is rather like telephoning. It is our line of communication with God. We can dial right through at any time and for any reason. Just as a telephone has a part for listening and a part for speaking, so we need to look upon prayer as a conversation we enjoy **with God** rather than a speech we make **to God.** God wants to speak to us equally as much as we desire to speak to Him. We need to watch that we do not have so much to say to God that He is unable to get a word in edgeways! Samuel said "Speak, for your servant is listening." (1 Sam.3.10) Our attitude is often the reverse. "Listen, Lord, your servant is speaking." Satan will steal the time we should give in prayer if we are not careful and disciplined. (Col. 4.2) This isolates us from God and imperils our spiritual life and witness.

(b) **Public Prayer** While it is important to have set times of prayer alone, it is also a great source of strength and blessing to pray with others. Too many neglect the prayer meeting and so deprive themselves and the church of blessing and progress.

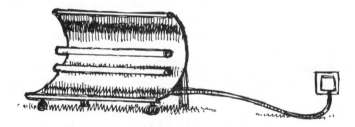

A famous preacher once asked a young man before the service if he would like to see the heating system in his large chapel. He was taken to the basement and shown a large group of people engaged in earnest prayer. Prayer is the switch that turns the fire on; it allows the warmth of God's love and the power of His Spirit to flow into the church. A church without a prayer meeting is like an electric fire switched off, it is cold and lifeless.

Peter knew the power of prayer. Because "many people had gathered and were praying" (Acts 12.12) he was delivered from prison. Paul sought the prayers of the churches and often sent them prayer requests, e.g. "Brothers, pray for us that the message of the Lord may spread rapidly and be honoured, just as it was with you. And pray that we may be delivered from wicked and evil men." (2 Thess.3.1,2) When the people of God pray, the preaching of His Word will prevail. We owe it to ourselves and we owe it to others to live a life of prayer. Samuel said "As for me, far be it from me that I should sin against the Lord by failing to pray for you." (I Sam.12.23)

If we continue steadfastly in these four vital activities we shall go on to see in our lives and fellowships the results that are mentioned in Acts 2.47. Our hearts will be full of praise to God. We shall experience goodwill amongst the people and see others converted through our witness.

May each reader of this book not only become a Christian and be baptized, but **continue** living the Christian life in fellowship with others and in an ever deepening relationship with Jesus Christ. While in Antioch, Paul and Barnabas spoke to the converts and 'urged them to **continue in the grace of God'.** Acts 13.43) They returned later "strengthening the disciples and encouraging them to remain true to the faith. 'We must go through many hardships to enter the kingdom of God' they said." (Acts 14.22)

QUESTIONS TO ANSWER
1. How can you make sure you will progress as a Christian and not go back to your old way of life?

....

....

....

2. What place should the Bible have in our lives?

....

....

....

3. Why is Christian fellowship so necessary?

....

....

....

4. Why should Christians 'break bread' together?

....

....

....

5. Why is prayer so important for the Christian?

....

....

....

APPENDIX 1

WHY IMMERSION

It has been assumed rather than taught in this booklet, that baptism is practised by immersing the candidate in water. Some of the reasons for this are listed below.

1. The Meaning Of The Word

The Greek verb 'baptizo' means to dip, to submerge. The Greeks used it to describe the dyeing of a garment, and the drawing of water by dipping a cup into a bowl. It would be necessary to immerse the entire garment if it was to be completely dyed and to put the cup beneath the water to fill it. In the Greek version of the Old Testament 'baptizo' is used of Naaman dipping himself in Jordan (2 Kings 5.14). Jesus Christ used the same word to indicate that He would be immersed in suffering and overwhelmed with judgment on the Cross (Lk.12.50).

2. The Practice Of The Jews

The Jews practised baptism by immersion. When a Gentile left behind his pagan beliefs and placed his faith in the living God, he could only become a worshipping member of the Jewish community by being baptized. The baptism had to take place in the presence of three witnesses; the individual had to declare his faith in the God of Israel; after which immersion took place. His past was considered to be forgotten while his present and future life were to be marked by a new relationship with God and His people.

3. The Baptism Of John

John the Baptist seems to have had a unique commission to baptize, "He who sent me to baptize with water" (Jn.1.33), and he obviously adapted Jewish baptism for his own particular mission. John preached the necessity of repentance for the remission of sins and then baptized those who turned to God, as a sign that the old life was finished and a new life begun. He baptized in Jordan, and is recorded as baptizing "at Aenon near Salim, because there was plenty of water, and people were constantly coming to be baptized." (Jn.3.23), which suggests immersion.

4. The Baptism Of Jesus Christ

Jesus Christ was baptized by John in the river Jordan, and undoubtedly was immersed in the same way as the Gentile converts and repentant Jews. Both Matthew and Mark record that Jesus 'went up out of the water' after He was baptized. The baptism of Jesus forms the link between John's baptism and Christian baptism.

When Jesus Christ stood in the river Jordan it was not as a repentant sinner, as John obviously sensed, but to 'fulfil all righteousness', that is, to do all that God required of Him. He was there taking the guilty sinner's place, identifying Himself with them in their relation to God as sinners. His baptism in water pointed clearly first to His death on the cross when He would again stand in the place of the sinner and then to His burial. His coming up from the water was a picture of His resurrection and ascension.

If we are baptized by immersion, we are surely following in the footsteps of the Master, which is a great privilege.

5. The Practice Of The Early Church
The most detailed account we have of a baptismal service in the book of Acts is that of the Ethiopian. (Acts 8.36-39) The relevant phrases are "Then both Philip and the eunuch went down into the water, and Philip baptized him. When they came up out of the water..." The early Christians would continue baptizing by immersion as it was the only form they knew.

6. The Teaching Of The Apostles
The classic passage is of course Rom.6.1-11 where Paul uses the terms death, burial and resurrection. He speaks of being "baptized into His death", "buried with Him through baptism" and "raised from the dead". When a person becomes a Christian, the sinner he once was is considered to be dead and buried, whereas the person he now is, is very much alive spiritually. The baptistry then becomes, in picture, an open grave for sinners, who are raised to live a new life in Christ. This has been more fully explained in the main section on baptism.

Baptism by immersion is the clearest and most appropriate way of expressing these wonderful truths.

APPENDIX 2
An Old Testament Picture Of Baptism (1 Cor.10.1-11)

In this section Paul makes a solemn warning to the complacent Christians at Corinth by referring to the history of the children of Israel. They experienced redemption when delivered from Egypt, baptism when passing through the sea and God's continual provision and protection as they journeyed through the wilderness. Yet because they returned to forbidden ways, nearly all of them perished in the wilderness. "These things happened to them as examples and were written down as warnings for us . . . so, if you think you are standing firm, be careful that you don't fall." (v.11). Let us heed the warning and live consistent Christian lives, or we will deprive ourselves of the rich blessing God longs to give us.

It was a unique experience for the children of Israel to pass through the Red Sea on dry land. With the water piled up on either side, and the cloud above them, they are described as having been "baptized into Moses in the cloud and in the sea". (v.2) As they came up out of the Red Sea, the waters closed behind them. This meant that they were free from the bondage of Egypt and the domination of Pharaoh. It also meant that they could not turn back. As the wilderness opened before them they began a new way of life with God, He guided them with the cloud and by the leadership of Moses. When we put our faith in Jesus Christ, He breaks the power of Satan's domination and frees us from the bondage of sin. "If the Son sets you free, you will be free indeed". (John 8.36) He opens up the way for fellowship with God, we are under His leadership and the guidance of the Holy Spirit. Baptism by immersion expresses for the Christian what the Red Sea meant for the Israelite, that the old way of life was finished and a new one had begun.

Sadly, they later returned to their former sinful ways so that we read "God was not pleased with most of them; their bodies were scattered over the desert." (v.5) Having begun a new life they failed to go through with it. After their deliverance from the Egyptians (Ex.14) their hearts were filled with praise and thanksgiving (Ex.15). A short while later they met difficulties such as lack of food and water. They then hankered after the life they had left instead of trusting God to provide for the journey ahead.

Our Christian pathway will not always be easy. Jesus Christ said "In this world you will have trouble. But take heart! I have overcome the world." (Jn.16.33) We must expect to be tempted by the enemy and tested by God. James encourages us to "Consider it pure joy, my brothers, whenever you face trials of many kinds, because you know that the testing of your faith develops perseverance. Perseverance must finish its work so that you may be mature and complete, not lacking anything." (Jas.1.2-4) When we meet difficulties we must not look for a way out but look for a way through with God's help. When we come through the trials, we shall have a firmer faith in God and be stronger Christians. If we had no problems our faith would be very anaemic. The trials God allows (as opposed to those we inflict on ourselves) are not a sign of His displeasure, but rather the reverse. Because He loves us, He tests us in order to make us richer in character and more established in our faith. (Read Heb.12.7-11)

APPENDIX 3
PRACTICAL DETAILS — FOR THOSE BEING BAPTIZED

1.   Having read this booklet and the relevant passages in the Bible, you may want to obey the command of Jesus Christ and be baptized. If this is so, then your next step is to express your desire to your minister or an elder in your church, who will discuss the arrangements with you as well as explain anything you do not understand.

2.   If the church to which you belong agrees to baptize you and you are still under age it will be necessary to have your parents' permis-

sion. Should you have any difficulties at home, a Christian from your church will always call and speak with your parents.

3.   Invite your family, relatives and friends to attend the service. It is an opportunity to show other people how much Jesus Christ means to you. Someone else may become a Christian or be baptized as a result of attending.

4.   You may want to think carefully about where the baptism is to take place. Some people are baptized in church buildings, others in a river or the sea, where many more will witness the service.

5.   Do wear suitable clothing. The person conducting the service will advise you on this and explain how everything takes place. If you have not previously witnessed a baptismal service, it would be wise to take the opportunity of attending one if possible.

6.   Ask a close friend to sit with you to support you on the night and to hand you a towel as you leave the water.

FOR THOSE BAPTIZING
1.   Explain carefully to those you are baptizing how you want them to stand, how you will hold them and all the practical details surrounding their entering and leaving the water. The more informed they are the more relaxed they will be.

2.   Make sure that a maximum amount of water is in the baptistry as this makes baptizing so much easier.

3.   It is helpful, though not necessary to have 2 people doing the baptizing. This gives a greater sense of security to the person being baptized, as well as being easier in the event of a heavy person, or several people being baptized during the service.

4.   Do baptize slowly and gently as this gives greater dignity to this ordinance. Many baptize hurriedly and enthusiastically sending water in all directions. This tends to detract from the baptism, focusing people's minds on the 'splash' rather than the beautiful symbolism being portrayed. It also intimidates those thinking about baptism. This is a further reason for having 2 people to do the baptism.

5.   Always remember that a baptismal service will bring into the church many people who do not normally attend our places of worship. We want them to understand and value this important sacrament given to us by our Lord Jesus Christ. Ensure that everything is done decently and in order.

6.   Ask for refreshments to be available at the end of the service. This will create a relaxed atmosphere in which church members can meet and share with those attending for the first time.

7.   Encourage the church to pray for those who have been baptized in the following week, as they will be special targets for Satanic attacks. (see Matt. 3.16-4.11).

SOME FURTHER READINGS ON BAPTISM

In the Gospels
Baptism of John: Mt.3.1-12; Mk.1.1-8; Lk.3.1-20; Jn.1.15-28.
Baptism of Jesus: Mt.3.13-17; Mk.1.9-11; Lk.3.21-22; Jn.1.29-34

In the Acts
Baptism of the Ethiopian: Acts 8.26-40
Baptism of Saul: Acts 9.18,19
Baptism of Cornelius and others: Acts 10.47,48
Baptism of Lydia and her household; Acts 16.14,15
Baptism of the jailor and his household: Acts 16.25-34
Baptism of the Corinthians: Acts 18,8
Baptism of John's disciples: Acts 19.1-7

In the Epistles
Rom.6.1-11. 1 Cor.10.1-15. Gal.3.27. Col.2.12,13. 1 Pet.3.18-22.